"TWO WORDS"

"That Can Change Your Life Forever"

By Bishop Timothy W. Cummings

"TWO WORDS"
"That Can Change Your Life Forever"

By Bishop Timothy W. Cummings

Copyright 2019 by New Creations Chapel, Inc.

Published by New Creations Chapel, Inc.
PO Box 777
Richmond, IN 47375
(765) 935-2790

Acknowledgement

I am what I am today because of great people in my life like my wife of over 55 years, Bonnie L. Cummings; my Pastor, Dr. Raymond Rothwell; and my secretary since 2014, Lisa Patterson.

To my true love, Bonnie, what you have done to make this book possible is a true miracle in itself. Your love, encouragement, our loss of time together while I was working on it, your corrections and guidance on it have not been lost on me. Thank you my love!

Thank you, Dr. Raymond Rothwell, for all the encouragement and help you gave me to make this book possible.

Thank you, Lisa, for all the hours you spent going over our manuscript and making this book a reality. There are no words that can thank you enough for your labor.

I would also like to thank my good friend, Douglas Gerber, for his input.

A special thank you to my son, Matthew Cummings for his assistance.

Bishop Timothy W. Cummings

I have known Bishop Timothy W. Cummings and his wife Bonnie for many years, and I can assure you that they have had many "God Moments" where they needed a word or two from someone to get them into a place of victory. I can attest that those two words referred to in the title of this book, "Two Words" have affected their lives in many situations.

This is not just a book of the life of Tim & Bonnie Cummings. It is a book showing the reader that even when you have a Godly calling on your life, even a "Five-Fold Ministry Calling" found in Ephesians Chapter 4, Verses 11 and 12, there will be times that you need the "Two Words" in this book. When you have a personal, physical, financial, or spiritual need in your life, "Two Words" and its contents will help you find a way for you to have a **"Two Words"** moment this book describes.

Dr. Raymond E. Rothwell

Contents

Chapter One

"Two Words"

"Observe and hear all these words which I command thee, that it may go well with thee, and with thy children after thee for ever, when thou doest that which is good and right in the sight of the Lord thy God." **(Deuteronomy 12:28, KJV).**

There are "Two Words" from the Bible that, if you use, can change your life forever.

These "Two Words" were used together 44 times in the King James Version of the Bible.

My wife, Bonnie, and I have used these "Two Words" thousands and thousands and thousands of times.

In fact, these "Two Words" are synonymous in everything we do.

I started using these "Two Words" before I even realized they were in the Bible together.

If you were in the Church and Mission Ministries we were in, working with youth in transition, you would have used these "Two Words" all the time too!

Bonnie and I have had an unusual calling from God. We were called in 1969 and lead by God to have a Church, for all, that focused on Youth, ages 13-23, and Ministers that led

Churches, Mission Organizations, and Christian Organizations for 47 years.

Our ministry started as a local area Christian Choir that traveled around the eastern part of the United States singing and ministering at other Churches and Christian organizations. We grew into a Church with a residential boarding school on the Youth side and on the Ministers side we would counsel them, listen to the difficulties they were having as Ministers and help their Churches raise funds for Church projects.

We had approximately 250 youth that lived with us in our personal home and at New Creations Chapel's facility, prior to the boarding school, over an eleven year period.

We lived on the Indiana and Ohio state line in what we called the brick house, located on top of a big hill on the Indiana side, with our three children (Matthew, Natalie and Mark). Later we moved 1,500 feet east to the Ohio side of the property into what we called the white house, because it was white, where our fourth child, Jason, was born.

I remember a funny story while living in the white house, the boarding school boys lived with us at that time and one day my son, Mark, was watching television. He hollered to Bonnie, "Hey Mom, they just announced the White House is going to be on TV. Mom, are we going to be on TV!"

In all, we had an estimated 6,000 + youth in our residential boarding school over the 47 years at New Creations while we were on the hill and at the white house.

The first seven years of the ministry we had many youth from Wayne County Indiana and Preble County Ohio attend, what we called, the New Creations Choir meetings. Many of these youth found Jesus as their Lord and Savior. We had such great times singing in churches, going to camps and traveling. We continued with the choir up to the day we closed our campus at 6400 National Road East in Richmond, Indiana. Though in the latter days we didn't travel as far or as much.

While I was on the road with the choir, our Church was ministered to by our Associate Pastor, Larry Thomas, who was with us for 33 years.

The reason I said we used the "Two Words" so much is because of all the difficulties we ran into ministering to, what was at times, as many as 70 youth in transition, at home and on the road.

Without the "Two Words" we would have never seen so many souls give their heart to Jesus Christ!

We baptized in water by total submersion; adults, youth and children as we watched them yield their lives to Jesus Christ as their Lord.

We also had many who wanted more in the Lord, Jesus Christ, and were baptized in the Baptism of the Holy Ghost.

Yes, the "Two Words" were used all the time in our uncommon calling.

Chapter Two

"Not Going to Amount to Anything"

"For they being ignorant of God's righteousness, and going about to establish their own righteousness, have not submitted themselves unto the righteousness of God." **(Romans 10:3, KJV).**

These "Two Words" became a way of life for Bonnie and me because we were on a Godly faith walk. *"Now faith is the substance of things hoped for, the evidence of things not seen."* **(Hebrews 11:1, KJV).**

These "Two Words" have been used in every critical moment of our lives.

Everyone reading this has probably used these "Two Words" but may not have connected them as being used in the Bible together. Some of you may have even heard these "Two Words" preached about at some point in time.

These "Two Words" are an authoritative summary of our faith and our doctrine. *"Knowing that a man is not justified by the works of the law, but by the faith of Jesus Christ, even we have believed in Jesus Christ, and not by the works of the law: for by the works of the law shall no* flesh be justified."* **(Galatians 2:16, KJV).**

These "Two Words" are a visible sign of something invisible in our lives.

"Through faith we understand that the worlds were framed by the word of God, so that things which are seen were not made of things which do appear." **(Hebrews 11:3, KJV).**

These "Two Words" were (and continue to be) a symbol of our Christian walk while we ministered for the first 47 years at New Creations Chapel's campus. In fact, from day one of when we were born again these "Two Words" became the way we lived every moment of our lives.

I have a disturbing and life altering recollection of when I was in 10th grade at Fountain City High School. My teacher said to me, "You aren't going to amount to anything in your life."

A Christian teacher!

Before I was saved!

Before I knew God!

That teacher said I wasn't going to amount to anything!

Yes, I *needed* these "Two Words" before I was even 18 years old. The "Two Words" would propel me into the person I would become.

I believe my acting out in class and causing her trouble were the reasons she said that to me. Really what was happening was that I was crying out; **"I need help, someone help me!"** I didn't have those "Two Words" at that time and boy was I a mess.

When youth are experiencing a problem, we should never tell them they won't amount to anything. We should try to find out what's going on with them. A lot of times we get upset and we say something destructive or act ugly when someone acts out, causes problems, makes rude statements or asks a rude question. Before you pay a wrong with a wrong, why not try to see what's behind the acting out?

What's the reason behind the person causing the problems?

What's the reason behind the crude statement?

What's the reason behind the rude question?

See, I believe it's never right to purposely do wrong and never wrong to purposely do right.

Every youth from age 13-23 are transitioning from childhood to adulthood. They are in transition from having no God in their lives to having God in their lives or rejecting God in their lives. This seems to be a most critical stage in their lives for them to accept Jesus Christ to be their Lord or continue into adulthood lost, where the odds of them accepting salvation diminishes.

The "Two Words" we are going to share with you shortly, will help you to understand the youth or young adult that is acting out. Generally it is someone screaming; "Help me! Please help me!" I know I was screaming that out as a child and young adult.

Did you know that some people never become adults emotionally and are stuck in that transition? They start drugs, rebelliousness and/or acting out and they continue to remain the same age emotionally as they were when they started the sin.

"Please help me!" The only way we get them to transition is to find their need and help them become independent of their drug addiction, rebelliousness and/or acting out.

For ages 13-23 in transition, they need help to escape the problems that put them in that situation.

Chapter Three

From Battle to Battle to Blessing

"Not rendering evil for evil, or railing for railing: but contrariwise blessing; knowing that ye are thereunto called, that ye should inherit a blessing." **(1 Peter 3:9, KJV).**

The reason we need the "Two Words" is because life is one battle after another. Generally, it's not our doing; it's just LIFE! We have two choices; God's way or the thief's (devil's) way.

As a married man, I believe every time I go through a battle my wife also goes through the battle. The battles are with our enemy, the thief of life; the devil. But we should never render evil for evil. If someone treats you with hatred, you should try blessing them. The thief comes to steal from us! The thief wants to destroy our very presence on earth! Jesus says, *"The thief cometh not, but to steal and to kill, and to destroy..."* **(John 10:10, KJV).**

But when we use the special "Two Words" it activates the last part of **(John 10:10, KJV)** *"...I am come that they might have life, and that they might have it more abundantly."*

I love to activate the "Two Words" God has given us to overcome a devil that can no longer:

Steal from me;

Kill my dreams and visions; or

Destroy the works of God in my life.

Again, I believe every time Bonnie and I go through a battle, before we can reach God's abundant way of life or the more abundance that God has for us, we must overcome the devil by using the "Two Words" that I'm going to reveal to you, and then, wait for the blessing.

After every battle, comes the blessing to those of us who love the Lord. 'The bigger the battle the bigger the blessing.'

So, don't get upset at the battles of life. If you continue reading this book the "Two Words" to use will be revealed and if you use them you will be able to move into your abundant blessing and a much fuller life.

Sometimes it seems as if we must go through the pits of hell to get to the next abundance or the next blessing. *"And I say unto thee, That thou art Peter, and upon this rock I will build my church; and the gates of hell shall not prevail against it."* **(Matthew 16:18, KJV)**.

The devil drags us through what seems like a keyhole forward then he loves to drag us through it again backwards. The thief is angry at us and wants to activate his stealing, killing and destroying activities in our lives.

He knows we're getting ready to do something big; inherit some big blessing from God because we don't render evil for evil or railing for railing!

If we let him, the thief, will get us down and stomp on us. During those times if we use these "Two Words" that I'm about to reveal to you they will absolutely upset his methods, strategies and his wicked ways.

We can use these "Two Words" every day of our lives.

These "Two Words" are a symbol of the way Bonnie and I live. In fact, when we wake up in the morning the thief thinks to himself 'Oh no, Pastor Tim or Pastor Bonnie is awake and is going to destroy my plans.'

The thief wants to stop us from obtaining God's vision for our lives. He wants to prevent us from receiving the abundance God has for our lives.

If we will activate the "Two Words" we will activate God's blessings, God's abundance and a life worth living. The glory that only God can reveal to us. *"For I reckon that the sufferings of this present time are not worthy to be compared with the glory which shall be revealed in us."* **(Romans 8:18, KJV).**

The thought that we won't have sufferings to enable us to beat the thief is a lie from the thief. Let's not buy into the lie from the thief, the devil, the father of lies. *"Ye are of your father the devil, and the lusts of your father ye will do. He was a murderer from the beginning, and abode not in the truth, because there is no truth in him. When he speaketh a lie, he speaketh of his own: for he is a liar, and the father of it."* **(John 8:44, KJV).**

Then when we do go through something and suffer we will realize the thief cannot hurt us and our suffering is only a bump in the road to victory.

The "Two Words" that I will share with you must become a way of life for you to really receive the true value they will bring into your life when you start using them. Bring on the battles so we can obtain the abundance of blessings God has for us here on this earth. God, we need those "Two Words."

Chapter Four

Jesus Needed the "Two Words"

"(To the chief Musician for the sons of Korah, A Song upon Alamoth.) God is our refuge and strength, a very present help in trouble." **(Psalm 46:1, KJV).**

The "Two Words" that come from God is what Jesus needed to carry out His mission. God used those "Two Words" when He raised Jesus from the dead. You've read it time and time again. Get this in your heart. The next time the devil attacks you, use these "Two Words" and shout them out of your mouth with the power of God!

"And though they found no cause of death in him, yet desired they Pilate that he should be slain." **(Acts 13:28, KJV).**

No legal reason would stop Jesus' accusers. Yet, they wouldn't kill Him themselves. They would ask Pilate to do their dirty work for them. They didn't have a legal reason to kill Him and they didn't care.

"And when they had fulfilled all that was written of him, they took him down from the tree, and laid him in a sepulcher." **(Acts 13:29, KJV)**

We know it was prophesied that Jesus would have to die. He would have to go to the cross. Not for His sins; but for my sins, your sins, our sins. Jesus was a perfect sacrifice for us; no blemish, no sin. Yet, He had the sin of the world laid upon Him, for you and for me.

Yes, the accusers thought they had won the battle, that Jesus was dead! They thought it was all over. They forgot something. The "Two Words."

They manipulated Pilate to order His death. They took Him off the cross and put Him in a tomb. The believers and accusers thought He was defeated. They failed to remember one thing that was going to change the course of the world as well as our lives and many of your lives. The "Two Words that would raise Jesus from the grave!

The "Two Words" I am about to give you are from the Word of God. *"Every word of God is pure: he is a shield unto them that put their trust in him."* **(Proverbs 30:5, KJV)**.

The "Two Words" are the truth from the Word of God and they work in us that believe to change the course of our lives. *"For this cause also thank we God without ceasing, because, when ye received the word of God which ye heard of us, ye received it not as the word of men, but as it is in truth, the word of God, which effectually worketh also in you that believe."* **(1Thessalonians 2:13, KJV)**.

Chapter Five

Those "Two Words,"
"BUT GOD"

"But God raised him from the dead:" **(Acts 13:30, KJV).**

"BUT GOD!"

Those are the "Two Words" the devil doesn't want to hear come out of our mouths.

Our Lord and Savior, Jesus, needed God, the Father, to step in and raise Him from the dead. *"And he was seen many days of them which came up with him from Galilee to Jerusalem, who are his witnesses unto the people."* **(Acts 13:31, KJV)**.

Jesus was seen by many people for 40 days as proof that He had a "But God" moment.

Those words, "But God," would also resurrect Bonnie & me time and time again from troubles, problems and difficulties that would shape our faith and our lives into what they are today. I never dreamed those "Two Words" would have such an effect on us. The devil would shove us into a corner and a "But God!" moment would happen.

I remember one time when we were in a corner because of the devil and we just didn't know what to do.

We were in the process of building a gymnasium at 6400 National Road East, that later became our Church. It was an 80' x 100' building and 22' 6" high. We were also erecting a 60' x 100' school that was 10' high.

We ran out of money and had many children to feed. That was a difficult moment in our lives. There we were, a man and woman, called by God, who had sold all they had to reach youth for Jesus; and we were failing. I began thinking of someone who could possibly help us. I had no pride left. I was desperate. Someone came to mind and I thought, I'll just go ask. So I hopped in my car and drove to Liberty, Indiana. I was going to speak to a man who had been a big donor to us in the past.

After arriving at his home, I said to him, "I need $10,000 or we will have to shut down the ministry. He sat with tears in his eyes and said to me, "I have been praying and God told me *not* to give you the money."

Now, what would you think? A man who had donated large amounts of money to us in the past telling me 'GOD told him *not* to give you the money'.

Unbeknownst to me that was going to be a "But God" moment. Although at the time I was crushed, that would become the greatest lesson I would ever learn.

We had 24 hours to come up with $10,000. I was so desperate for funds that I was sobbing uncontrollably. A female Wayne County Sheriff's Deputy pulled me over and asked me what was wrong. She talked to me and helped me pull myself together.

When I arrived back in Richmond, I stopped at the post office to pick up the mail. I don't know if any of you reading this were in Richmond, Indiana right then and heard my screams but many of the postal workers did and they came running to see what was happening.

BUT GOD! He showed up!

And how He showed up!

GOD had delivered the money!

I hope you know the devil doesn't want you to make it!

"BUT GOD" wants to abundantly bless those who sell out to Jesus Christ as their Lord, King and Savior.

Bonnie and I have had "But God" moments again, and again throughout our lives and ministry. There have been many times when it looked as though we would have to close the ministry and it would collapse and die, "But God!"

Chapter Six

No Date with My Mate

"And said, For this cause shall a man leave father and mother, and shall cleave to his wife: and they twain shall be one flesh?" **(Matthew 19:5, KJV).**

A classmate of ours, Jim, told me that I would never get a date with my now wife, Bonnie L. (Reeves) Cummings. In fact, he bet me $20 that I would never get a date with her or ever get to kiss her. Back in 1960 that was a lot of money. I was motivated.

I wasn't saved then but Bonnie was, she was a true Christian. God was a big part of her life. I was a heathen, a non-believer, He was not a part of my life. But I had enough pride I thought it would be an easy $20.

The course of my life was about to change forever and I didn't even know it. See, the Bible had an answer for my pride, but at the time it was the last book I ever wanted to read. *"Pride goeth before destruction, and an haughty spirit before a fall."* **(Proverbs 16:18, KJV).**

As a heathen the only things I understood was from the devil. *"For the world offers only a craving for physical pleasure, a craving for everything we see, and pride in our achievements and possessions. These are not from the Father, but are from the world."* **(1 John 2:16, NLT).**

God will never accept our prideful boastings. So, Bonnie put me in my place by saying "NO!" Many times.

Every chance I got I dated other girls from all the surrounding towns. I was having fun dating and getting to kiss girls.

Kissing was as far as it went. Back then sex was something thought of by most of us as off limits until we were married.

Bonnie was dating a guy and he had asked her to go steady. That was another obstacle in my way. I had to come up with a strategy to get a date with that beautiful brown eyed girl.

All through school Bonnie had been a fat little farm girl. We kids were cruel and would make fun of her by singing:

"Our Bonnie lies over the ocean, our Bonnie lies over the sea; so, *don't* bring our Bonnie back to me."

We, the boys in our 1962 class, treated her so badly. She wanted nothing to do with us.

At the beginning of 10th grade when Bonnie came to school; she was a "knock out!" The boys in our class went crazy over her and that made her even more desirable to me and more determined to get a date with her.

I needed the "Two Words" from the Bible more than ever and God would activate them for me before I was even saved. But, I had to get around the following problems:

I was a heathen!

Bonnie was a Christian!

Bonnie was going steady with someone else!

I needed a "But God" moment in my life to even get a date with her. She was full of Jesus Christ. As a heathen, I needed Jesus but I didn't know it at the time.

I realized I was *in love* with Bonnie and wanted to marry her, so I told Jim to forget the bet. And I came up with a strategy. I would show up at her house when her boyfriend dropped her off. That way it would look as if she were expecting me. I started attending Church so it would look as if I had become a Christian. Lastly, I began to show her I was crazy in love with her by sending her flowers and cards.

Bonnie did everything to try to get rid of me.

She chased me away!

She tried to avoid me!

She ignored me.

She tried to fix me up with other girls.

She even tried to fix me up with her cousin!

I heard 'no' so many times; she wanted *nothing* to do with me! But it only made me more determined.

I didn't understand this was a "But God" moment in my life and that if I could overcome it I would become saved (born again) and in the end be called into the ministry as a Pastor, then Bishop overseeing other Pastors and men and women of God!

"But God" moments in our lives are moments that can change the way we live, the way we act and what we can become by accepting the "But God" moment for what it really is for us. It is a chance for us to change our character into a Godly person. A blood bought, blood washed of our sins, and a person going to heaven and not hell.

Finally, after six months it worked. I got a date, but only if my heathen parents and family were around.

It wouldn't be easy sailing with her. Bonnie wanted to know if I knew God, so I attended church but I wasn't saved. After a while she began to believe I was but I was still as lost as a goose; a heathen!

I was madly in love with Bonnie and I believed she loved me too or she would have never said yes when I asked her to marry me.

Then, on our wedding day, Neva Freeman, my Sunday School Teacher for many years, cornered me just like she did on my first day of Sunday school. It aggravated me so. Practically every time I saw her, she would say, "You'd be alright if you were a Christian." That used to drive me crazy! On that day she told me I needed Jesus Christ as Lord of my life.

I went behind the Church and smoked some cigarettes, while praying as a sinner, to not let Bonnie find out. I loved her as much as you can love a person without God showing you what love really is.

This "But God" moment was another example of what can happen to a man or woman who is lost and searching and doesn't even know what God has for their life. Yet, on that beautiful day God permitted me to marry the love of my life, the one who would be my life partner, my best friend, and lover now for over 56 + years. It truly is a love story of how, if we let it, "But God" will take us on a journey that was and is so, so beautiful, sweet, and loving even in the tough times of life.

Pray that you will have "But God" moments in your life that will bring you as much love, peace, happiness and joy that any person can have. Even without acknowledging God, I had a "But God" moment that changed my life forever.

Chapter Seven

"But God" Moments

"God is our refuge and strength, a very present help in trouble." **(Psalms 46:1, KJV).**

Back when we were building the school and gymnasium I was standing on the right corner of the gymnasium building; 22'6" off the ground, while the trusses were being delivered. One of those trusses came out of nowhere and hit me. I don't know how but I found myself holding on to that truss. It should have knocked me off and I should have fell and been severely injured or killed. "But God," saved me!

You know all these "But God" moments are teaching moments. We have learned to walk in faith when it seems like we aren't going to make it. *"(For we walk by faith, not by sight :)"* **(2 Corinthians 5:7, KJV).**

We have learned to trust God; not to trust reasoning or our understanding, but to acknowledge God. He's the one that directs our way. *"Trust in the Lord with all your heart; and lean not to your own understanding. In all thy ways acknowledge him, and he shall direct thy paths."* **(Proverbs 3:5, KJV).**

I remember one night a man came to the church and he said, "I'm Jesus." I replied, "You don't look like Jesus to me and I know

Him personally." I prayed with the guy and he left. The next day I was in the basement of the brick house on the campus of New Creations where at the time we had our office. The guy from the night before came down the stairs and he said he had been mistaken the night before. He said, "I'm Allah." I replied, "You missed it again." He took off after me and before I even had time to think he picked me up and threw me about 5' into the air. Now, I was a little guy compared to him. So I was thinking he was going to kill me. I got to my feet and he rushed me. I stated, "You won't touch me, in the Name of Jesus." I was thinking; ok God it's up to you now. He was coming at me; suddenly he stopped! He got so close to me I could smell his breath and it wasn't pleasant; it was a downright rank odor.

I just had another "But God" moment in my life. Every one of you have had one too. When you are backed into a corner and it looks like there's no way out, that's when you scream, "But God!"

It took an Indiana State Trooper, Rick Thalls who was a Wayne County Sheriff's Deputy, Pastor Henry Howells, Susan Sparks and myself to take that mans' hand off the gun he had taken from the deputy who had come to arrest him. This "But God" moment also saved my life.

You don't work 47 years in a ministry with youth who are in transition from teen to adult, who have some problems in their lives, and not have "But God" moments.

My wife, Bonnie, had a "But God" moment one time when one of our students stole a knife from the kitchen. He was threatening another student with it and Bonnie just stepped right in between them. I didn't know what she was thinking, but she took that knife away from the student. "But God" was in that situation also.

I'm telling you our Lord and Savior had a "But God" moment when God raised Him from the dead! He took on our sins!

Our depressions!

Our problems!

Our troubles!

God the Father raised Jesus, the Son, out of the grave. He can raise you out of whatever bad situation you get into as well.

"But God" raised me, Bishop Timothy W. Cummings, to be somebody in a world that said I was going to be nobody. If that 10th grade teacher would have told me at that particular time in my life that I could amount to something, maybe it wouldn't have taken me so long to get saved. People who said I'd never amount to anything forgot the "But God" moments that would come into my life.

I say to you from the day you are born, you will have "But God" moments!

What a "But God" life; from a heathen to a Bishop in God's service.

Chapter Eight

God's Plan of Action

"For I know the thoughts that I think toward you, saith the Lord, thoughts of peace, and not of evil, to give you an expected end." **(Jeremiah 29:11, KJV).**

The following is a text message I sent to my employees and Church leaders in the fall of 2018:

"Yesterday I may have seemed a little upset; I was. I got a notice from Reid Hospital that I had a spot on my lung. It could be nothing or it could be cancer. I ask that you pray it is nothing, but if it is something to be concerned about, that God will heal it in the Name of Jesus.

God's plan of action that He would give to me: Aggressively try to find the problem then fight it.

I have an appointment this Thursday with my doctor to lay out a plan. Yes, this is a "But God" moment. I must believe and trust in God more than ever before. If the spot is not a problem, then I will be the loudest person praising God on earth. If the spot is a problem, then I will be the loudest person praising God for a miracle healing on earth.

Your future with New Creations has never been brighter. I plan to carry out the vision God has given me; to establish an

International Headquarters and local Church here in Richmond for our international and local ministries and to continue my calling to help and guide ministries and youth ages 13-23 and to be a blessing in starting and helping Churches, missions and Christian organizations.

This spot on my lung is only an attack from the devil. As you know he wants to steal, kill and destroy us; to wipe us off the face of the earth.

We will attack back establishing this International and local ministry, whose purpose is to have a Church that focuses on making others successful, and our work will be working through others. Let us determine more now than ever before that we will truly have a Matthew 5:16 Ministry. "Let your light shine before men that they will see our good works for God and glorify our Heavenly Father." **(Matthew 5:16, KJV).**

Sickness or not we will establish for all of you (when He calls me home) to take over this Ministry to make others successful in their calling. We will not quit or slow down but get stronger in Jesus Christ. Yes, our first step seems to have been slowed down, but let us fight to bring glory to God.

About Bonnie's health; she seems to still have the original problems. We are sick and tired of the devil beating up on her. We are going to be more aggressive to find the underlying reason for her spiked fevers, elevated heart rate, ear infections, tiredness and sickness.

Enough is enough! We are praying we live to be 120 years old and in good health, doing God's glorious work."

Bonnie was able to schedule an appointment with a doctor in Indianapolis and we got a second opinion. She was healed in Jesus name. *"Who his own self bare our sins in his own body on the tree, that we, being dead to sins, should live unto righteousness: by whose stripes ye were healed."* **(1Peter 2:24, KJV).**

We must remember these are "But God" moments! *"Which in time past were not a people, but are now the people of God: which had not obtained mercy, but now have obtained mercy."* **(1 Peter 2:20, KJV).**

We will fight hard for our calling of helping others to be successful in God's work and to be saved and filled by the mighty hand of the Holy Ghost. We will not stop, bend or bow to this enemy of our flesh and soul. So, let's get our "But God" moves of God going and growing to bring glory to Him for our healing touches from God!

We get those "But God" moments by repenting. *"And the times of this ignorance God winked at; but now commandeth all men every where to repent:"* **(Acts 17:30, KJV).**

We get our "But God" moments from Jesus Christ who loves us and died for us. *"But God, who is rich in mercy, for his great love wherewith he loved us,"* **(Ephesians 2:4, KJV)** *"But God commandeth his love toward* *us, in that, while we were yet sinners, Christ died for us."* **(Romans 5:8, KJV).**

The enemy never knows when we Christians are going to say enough is enough! Do not let the devil tell you anything else!

The spot on my lung was nothing but something designed to cause fear. "But God" wants me to continue seeing miracle after miracle and guiding youth, children and adults, ministers, Churches and mission organizations to their full potential.

I believe the youth we have helped in the past, are helping in the present, will help in the future and will have "But God" moments and carry on our calling!

To God be the glory!

Chapter Nine

"But God" People!

"But he was wounded for our transgressions, he was bruised for our iniquities: the chastisement of our peace was upon him; and with his stripes we are healed." **(Isaiah 53:5, KJV).**

Bonnie and I have had the privilege to work with many ministers that I would qualify as "But God" men and women. These wonderful people of God, many of whom, looked like they were down for the last count, risking their finances, their ministries, everything they had, yet they would not quit unless God told them to quit. They would not give up on God for any reason.

We have a friend who pioneered a work of God in the men's prison system. She worked with what I would call the worst of the worst. "But God." This woman of God answered the call to go into the prison. If you knew or met her you would think, what in the world is that sweet petite lady doing going into a prison and ministering to these unruly men?

She has had to face many "But God" moments in her life. Her husband of 50 years was unexpectedly called home to be with Jesus. He had worked with her in the prison well into his 70's when he suddenly died. She went right back to volunteering and ministering without even giving it a second thought. Now that was a "But God" moment in her life. She still goes several times a week to minister in an all-male prison and, yes, the devil has attacked her; "But God" won.

Her husband went to heaven, but she continues to lead many lost men to the Lord. She is always so excited to see those men give their lives to Jesus. She is giving hope to the prisoners who have no hope. She helps them find Jesus as the Lord and Savior of their lives.

This woman of God had another "But God" moment when just weeks after the death of her husband she had a terrible accident and was immobile with several broken bones. This "But God" woman can never be counted out because of her faith. She believes God's Word! She was laid up in bed for about a year with the devil trying to defeat her. She would not give up or give in and she gave all the glory to God for her healing. Like most soldiers of the Lord she returned to the men's prison ministry and brought the Word of God to even more prisoners. She has overcome extraordinary circumstances to be able to continue ministering to those lost and sometimes forsaken men. 'The greater the call, the greater the challenges.

This noble, "But God" woman has been challenged again and been diagnosed with lung cancer. At first she only shared this with her family and the closest of friends. This is another "But God" moment and she has trusted God through it all. When I told her I wanted to include her in this book she asked me not to use her name. Now that's a "But God" woman of God.

This lady is just one of many that are "But God" people willing to lay their lives down to carry out the calling God has given them. They do this without any glory but give all the glory to God. *"Let your light so shine before men, that they may see your good works, and glorify your Father which is in heaven."* **(Matthew 5:16, KJV).**

I see it like this; we will have many "But God" challenges and opportunities in life with health conditions that suggest we will die sick. We can't dictate to God but we have the right to quote His Word, believe His Word and stand on His Word. I don't believe we have to die sick or get sick to die. I believe God can take you home whenever He wants to. We are healed because the Word of God says we are healed and we just have to receive our healing. We are healed no matter how we feel, how we look or how many times our body tells us we are not healed. We are healed by the stripes of Jesus. *"But he was wounded for our transgressions, he was bruised for our iniquities: the chastisement of our peace was upon him; and with his stripes we are healed."* **(Isaiah 53:5, KJV)**.

Sickness is another chance for a "But God" moment in your life to overcome the devil. If you're born again with Jesus in your life "But God" moments will be just another bump in the road in your life for God to do great things; including healing.

Chapter Ten

Being a Natural and Spiritual Parent

"For though ye have ten thousand instructors in Christ, yet have ye not many fathers: for in Christ Jesus I have begotten you through the gospel." **(1 Corinthians 4:15, KJV).**

The moment you surrender and become born again you become a "But God" man or woman of God; you cannot be counted out. You are no longer a worldly person. You are an obedient person of God. You won't quit if you fail. When God tells you to close the door to something you love it may break your heart; you may cry many tears and may suffer much during that period. But if you're a "But God" person you'll do exactly what God tells you to do. You'll do it out of obedience and won't quit Jesus for any reason.

The moment you get saved and become a "But God" man or woman of God you become a Nehemiah symbol. *"So built we the wall; and all the wall was joined together unto the half thereof: for the people had a mind to work."* **(Nehemiah 4:6, KJV).**

I know Bonnie and I are having a little difficulty right now, but I know it's just another "But God" moment in our lives. My wife of 56 + years with whom I started first grade with at Fountain City Elementary School, would like to retire. She should be able to retire, but she has a husband whose calling is to instruct ministers and youth and be active in the ministry. I have been refreshed and recharged and am ready to carry on my calling of God to serve ministers and youth. I want to continue to reach out and serve ministers and youth until the day I die. I am trying to train others so when God calls me home the ministry can be carried on. I know this is not the end of Bonnie and me ministering together. It is a "But God" moment until we ascend to the next phase of our calling. We are trying to locate likeminded Christian Ministers and work through them so Bonnie and I can have time to rest, relax and enjoy ourselves and our family.

Bonnie is a mother to our own four precious children and a surrogate mother to the 250 youth who lived with us over the years. She is grandmother to seven adored grandchildren and three darling great grandchildren. Bonnie and I love being grandparents. This "But God" moment is practicing our calling to ministers, youth, our children, grandchildren and great grandchildren while still being a spiritual father and mother to so, so many.

We have also had many "But God" moments with our own children. Our son, Jason, who was born more than 42 years ago, was almost lost in childbirth. Doctors didn't have all the medical equipment and instruments then that they have today. As Jason was making his way down the birth canal his heartbeat went from 90 beats per minute to 80 and continued decreasing until it was finally down to 10 beats per minute. Our doctor took the nurse's hand, stood back against the wall, looked at me and said, "You know God and you know how to pray. It is now up to God." I don't know of any doctor that would do that today. As I stood there, everything in my life, my wife, my precious baby son, time itself stood still. We prayed and Jason began backing up through the birth canal. Then when he did emerge he had a red mark around his neck from where the umbilical cord had been wrapped around his neck. That was a "But God" moment. I believe because we were sold out to God, He performed a miracle for us. God looked down and decided this was going to be a "But God" moment. God took that umbilical cord from around our son's neck and he was still able to be born naturally. Let me tell you something, there is never a desperate time that prayer won't take care of and develop a "But God" moment. The moment you get saved you belong to God and you get a mind to work for Him. When you get God's mind to work, you get it after you've had some "But God" moments and realize God's in charge and when he gives an order, a sold out Christian carries it out!

I believe we will have many instructors in our lives. "But God" spiritual mothers and fathers who are called to do great ministries for God are few and must pay a great price to execute their calling. *"For though ye have ten thousand instructors in Christ, yet have ye not many fathers: for in Christ Jesus I have begotten you through the gospel."* **(1 Corinthians 4:15, KJV)**.

Chapter Eleven

I'll go into the Ministry

"So then neither is he that planteth any thing, neither he that watereth; but God that giveth the increase." **(1 Corinthians 3:7, KJV).**

I remember one time a man told me he would go into the ministry if he had four new tires for his car. I said to him, "Follow me." I took him to BF Goodrich. I told the guy behind the counter, "Give this guy four brand new tires." The man I was buying the tires for asked, "What are you doing?" I replied, "I'm buying you four new tires so you can go into the ministry." I never saw anyone run so fast in my life. He peeled out of that parking lot burning rubber. There he went speeding off to get out of going into the ministry. I didn't see him again for quite a long time.

Don't tell me you're going to go into the ministry if only... Don't you tell me something stands between you and the ministry! You tell me what obstacle stands between you and the ministry and I'll find a solution for you.

Young people tell me all the time, "Well, I've got school debt." I respond, "I've got a plan for that." They sputter and stutter and off they go. Did you know the government has a program that if you make a reasonable payment and work for a non-profit organization for ten years all your student debt can be forgiven? I told a kid that once and I haven't seen him for a while either. It's amazing what people will come up with to get out of God's calling.

You know if you have a "But God" moment in your life I believe you will have a mind to work for God some way or somehow. Yet, you are going to have some pit moments. I've learned that we're going to be in a pit just like Joseph was; a few times. And if you don't want to get into a pit, don't get into the ministry. And if you are in the ministry and haven't been in a pit yet, ha-ha, you'll be in one soon. *"And it came to pass, when Joseph was come unto his brethren, that they stript Joseph out of his coat, his coat of many colours that was on him; and they took him, and cast him into a pit: and the pit was empty, there was no water in it."* **(Genesis 37:23-24, KJV).**

You need a "But God" moment so you can be rescued from the pits of life. Life's problems; life's difficulties; life's troubles; the lack of finances and the many problems the devil will throw at you because you are in the ministry. I believe the moment you enter the ministry and you get rooted, you get raised to the next level of measure by the devil.

"I have planted, Apollos watered, but God gave the increase." **(1 Corinthians 3:6, KJV).**

You've got to get to the point where you realize that no increase happens until "But God" does it. No increase of money comes until "But God" makes it happen. Nothing happens until there's a "But God" situation starting. In those moments are when you are given the increase.

I know that you may have been extremely sick, had a terrible fever. That's a "But God" moment for you. That's a "But God" moment to move you into a new position of trusting God.

Every difficulty that comes into our lives, every situation that arrives in our life is a "But God" moment. We need those moments to be rescued out of those pits. If you go through the "But God" moments in life with God, you can claim health, love, freedom, grace and all the things of God. These belong to the "But God" people of God and He will give you the power to get it. *"But thou shalt remember the Lord thy God: for it is he that giveth thee power to get wealth, that he may establish his covenant which he sware unto thy fathers, as it is this day."* **(Deuteronomy 8:18, KJV)**.

Not only does God give the "But God" people of His power to get wealth when they go through the "But God" moments in life, He also gives them the ability to give to others, which returns to them double if they do it scripturally. You've got to give to get double. You've got to have the right motive. You give to get, knowing that God is in charge of your money, your life and everything you have! *"Give and it shall be given unto you; good measure, pressed down, and shaken together, and running over, shall men give into your bosom. For with the same measure that ye mete withal it shall be measure to you again."* **(Luke 6:38, KJV)**.

Chapter Twelve

A Doubled Life

"And the Lord turned the captivity of Job, when he prayed for his friends: also the Lord gave Job twice as much as he had before." **(Job 42:10, KJV).**

"But as for you, ye thought evil against me; but God meant it unto good, to bring to pass, as it is this day, to save much people alive." **(Genesis 50:20, KJV).**

I believe God has called Bonnie and me to help other ministers when they go through their terrible "But God" moments because we understand what they are going through. We felt that pain when we had to close New Creations Christian Boarding School, Church, College, Camp, Horse Barn and Campus. I can feel their heartache when they have that moment. Why, because I've been through it. I've felt it. I've tasted it. When you call me for prayer, I lay in agony sometimes; for you.

A minister down in Florida, an older gentleman, with lots of difficulties, wants to attain a Church building. He asked me to be his pastor and help him with this endeavor. He is a member of Faith Christian Fellowship International (FCFI) of which I am Bishop; I'm believing a "But God" moment for him.

Joseph Cummings, no relation to us, wants to be in the ministry. He used to work for us in our IT department and his mother was a Dorm Minister at New Creations. This is a young man that when he asked his, now wife, to marry him told her there was a condition. He said he had been called to be in the ministry and that it would be a part of their lives. When I hear these people who are eager to be about our Father's business my desire is to help them and not give them any chance to escape. If they do escape, it will be of their own doing; not mine. I will do whatever I can to help them.

We, as ministers, need to have "But God" moments for other people. We've got to quit building our own kingdoms and just our own facilities. I believe a lot of ministers do this and it is something we cannot afford to do in these latter days. We must help each other. I believe New Creations Chapel gives us a perfect way to do this. But I also believe every "But God" moment Bonnie and I have had has brought us to this point. TO SAVE MANY PEOPLE! See, that's what happened to Joseph. He went through all those "But God" times, being thrown into a pit, being falsely accused by Potiphar's wife, being falsely imprisoned and being forgotten after interpreting other's dreams. But he went through all of that to be able to save many people. That's what we're called to do. We are "But God" people to help save any who are alive in this time of our lives. *"And it came to pass, when his master heard the words of his wife, which she spake unto him, saying, After this manner did thy servant to me; that his wrath was kindled. And Joseph's master took him, and put him into the prison, a place where the king's prisoners were bound: and he was there in the prison."* **(Genesis 39:19-20, KJV).**

Most people counted us out when we closed the doors of New Creations campus. Well, just watch out; you haven't seen anything yet.

We obeyed God in the past and will obey Him in the future. I believe we will see more people come to Jesus Christ in our latter years than in our former. In fact, I'll prophesy this: I've witnessed thousands of people come to Christ, yet, I believe I will see more people won to Christ in one year in this ministry than I saw won in all the 47 years in the past ministry. It's because all of the "But God" moments that we've experienced and we gave God all the glory.

I believe God is going to double us just like he did Job. *"And the Lord turned the captivity of Job, when he prayed for his friends: also the Lord gave Job twice as he had before."* **(Job 42:10, KJV).**

New Creations Chapel (NCC) had 720 acres. I believe we will be blessed with 1, 440 acres.

NCC witnessed and ministered to over 6,000 youth. I believe we will witness and minister to over 12,000 youth.

NCC hosted over 15,000 campers. I believe we will host over 30,000 campers.

NCC had 125,000 sq. ft. of building space. I believe we will be blessed with 250,000 sq. ft. of building space.

NCC had 65 staff members. I believe we will be blessed with 130 staff members.

NCC sang with 49 + choir members. I believe we will be blessed with 98 + choir members.

NCC had one location. I believe we will be blessed with many locations.

NCC had one church. I believe we will be blessed with many churches.

NCC has helped many missionaries. I believe we will help double the missionaries.

NCC has helped many missions. I believe we will help with double the missions.

NCC had one cross. I believe we will display many crosses.

NCC has discipled many. I believe we will double our discipleship.

I would like to live to be 120 years old, *"And the Lord said, MY spirit shall not always strive with man, for that he also is flesh; yet his days shall be an hundred and twenty years."*
(Genesis 6:3, KJV), still be in good health and preaching while Bonnie plays music. I would like to see several crosses be erected all over the United States and the world. I would also like to see a discipleship program that will teach ministers so they can minister around the world. I would like to see discipleship programs for children, youth and adults that will also reach the world. *"Let your light so shine before men, that they may*

see your good works, and glorify your Father which is in heaven." **(Matthew 5:16, KJV).**

Don't get me wrong; I do not believe the ministry will be duplicated of what it was, but rather a ministry that through others, who walk beside us in this coming reign and move of God will be bigger and spread wider to reach more people.

The former had to die in order to return to us in another form. Our houses and businesses that had to be surrendered will be returned to us doubled, in Jesus name, with us being in good health until the day He calls us home.

The Word and the "But God" moments prior that have caused suffering will return with our good works, giving glory to God! Yes, a life with "But God!" moments.

You need "But God" moments.

"But God" moments will bring us to see many Churches started and many missionaries helped around the world. Don't underestimate the "Two Words," "But God" because God can change the world with just one spoken word!

Chapter Thirteen

Chosen by God!

"But God hath chosen the foolish things of the world to confound the wise; and God hath chosen the weak things of the world to confound the things which are mighty;" **(1 Corinthians 1:27, KJV).**

To be chosen by God to do anything at all is truly a miracle. The only way I have the ability and knowledge to carry out my calling is because God gives it and reveals it to me. Over the years God has chosen me to do some extraordinary things.

One of the first things God called me to do was to understand people who were searching for God; needing correction, Godly advice, helping to see the end of a project; all while having compassion, mercy and grace for others. I thank God He has shown me my gifts and put me in places to help others. *"But God hath revealed them unto us by his Spirit: for the Spirit searcheth all things, yea, the deep things of God."* **(1 Corinthians 2:10, KJV).**

God does the searching and if you have the fullness of the Holy Ghost, He reveals it to you. Wow! What a joy to be able to guide and direct others to see their gifts.

I know that God has chosen me by calling me to a very unusual calling; to counsel Ministers, youth and ministries. *"And he gave some, apostles; and some, prophets; and some, evangelists; and some, pastors and teachers;"* **(Ephesians 4:11, KJV).** *"And God hath set some in the church, first apostles, secondarily prophets, thirdly teachers, after that miracles, then gifts of healings, helps, governments, diversities of tongues."* **(1 Corinthians 12:28, KJV).**

In the first seven years of the ministry the Youth Choir was the focus with Ministers, Churches and Church related ministries (missions and Christian organizations) following. In the 40 years after our concentration and focus was on a boarding school and college for youth in transition with Ministers, Churches and Church related ministries following. As I have entered my senior years of life, God has again changed the order and focus of my ministry.

We were called on Thanksgiving Day, November of 1969, to our ministry and on November 2, 2019, we hosted our 50th year of implementing what God has called us to. We have watched God perform the "But God" moments in our lives when others thought we would not make it. With this "But God" time I feel like a spring chicken with the new excitement of the things God is going to do.

In the early years my heart was to have a Church that focused first on youth; Ministers were my second focus. "But God" changed that on July 7, 2016. It took me until February 1, 2018 to see the change, from being a church focused on youth to a Church focused on developing Ministers. I didn't understand the vision and change of focus until January of 2019. I didn't think I would ever work with youth again. "But God" has a plan. He just had to make me aware to direct my gifts to be a Church with a focus of Ministering, first to the development of Ministers and then focus on youth. I have always worked with both adults and children, however, now my primary focus will be to the development of Ministers who will reach out to youth.

I have learned what it says in 1 Corinthians, *"So then neither is he that planteth any thing, neither he that watereth; but God that giveth the increase."* **(1 Corinthians 3:7, KJV).**

If we are in the will of God, He will give the increase. It is God, and God alone, that gives the increase. We can make plans, but we better be in line with God so we can receive the increase.

Join us as we watch what "But God" miracles the Lord is going to implement in our Social Media Ministry, Newsletter Ministry, Book Ministry, Minister's Ministry, Youth Ministry, Broadcasting Ministry, Mission Ministry, Christian related Ministries and Church Ministry.

New Creations Chapel's purpose is:

1. Love God
   "Jesus said unto him, Thou shalt love the Lord thy God with all thy heart, and with all thy soul, and with all thy mind. This is the first and great commandment." **(Matthew 22:37-38, KJV).**

2. Love People
   "And the second is like unto it, Thou shalt love thy neighbor as thyself. On these two commandments hang all the law and the prophets." **(Matthew 22:39-40, KJV).**
3. Make Disciples
   "Go ye therefore, and teach all nations, baptizing them in the name of the Father, and of the Son, and of the Holy Ghost: Teaching them to observe all things whatsoever I have commanded you: and, lo, I am with you always, even unto the end of the world. Amen." **(Matthew 18:19-20, KJV).**
4. Bring Glory to God
   "Let your light so shine before men, that they may see your good works, and glorify your Father which is in heaven." **(Matthew 5:16, KJV).**

Our Church's focus will be on Ministers, Churches and Church related Ministries; not forsaking the children, youth and adults that God will send us in our local Church while we believe for double growth.

Our mission giving goal is to give $50,000 + annually. We will direct 60% of that to local missions and 40% to foreign and international missions. We will continue to believe to double our Mission giving as we grow and to one day be able to give millions.

Our cross goal is to build as many crosses possible locally, statewide, nationally and worldwide.

Our discipleship goals are to disciple people of all ages and develop Ministers to advance into the entire world to spread the gospel of Christ Jesus.

Our school goal is to build a Minister's Trade & Discipleship School (MTDS) for all those who God has chosen to be in the ministry and advance them all over the world to spread the gospel of Christ Jesus.

Our Church goal is to build Churches locally, nationally and throughout the world to reach the lost.

Our mission and missionary goal is to develop and aid in starting as many missions as possible to launch into the world to win souls for Christ Jesus.

Our Christian organization goal is to train, instruct, educate, coach and assist as many Christian organizations as possible to help aid in winning the lost to Christ Jesus.

It will take "But God" moments for all of our goals to occur for us to reach any part or to fulfil any of our visions. When you are chosen by God there can be many "But God moments in your journey with Him.

Chapter Fourteen

You Need "But God" Moments!

"So now it was not you that sent me hither, but God: and he hath made me a father to Pharaoh, the lord of all his house, and a ruler throughout all the land of Egypt" **(Genesis 45:8, KJV).**

There are times you will go on a 'wild goose chase;' that's what my dad used to say. Yes, God will steer you to do something to see if you trust him to lead you. So, this is my story about a trip that God sent me on just to see if I would trust Him. *"Trust in the Lord with all thine heart; and lean not unto thine own understanding."* **(Proverbs 3:5, KJV).**

So often we are sent on journeys by God to show Him if we are relying on His directions or our own.

In September of 2018, a young man that I am discipling, Joseph, told me he had discovered a property that he believed could possibly be where we would build our new Church. I believe with all my heart God was leading Joseph to another "But God" moment, just to see whose understanding he would rely on, his own or God's.

The property that God lead Joseph to was 725 Progress Drive in Richmond, Indiana. I didn't have much interest in the property, but, God continued to speak to Joseph, and in effect, Joseph continued to tell me about it. Eventually we checked into it. It had three nice sized rooms and seemed to be just what we had been looking for. The address contained a seven in it and one of the interior doors even had a cross pattern on it. It was at a good location and affordable enough that we could purchase it and remain debt free.

A bank owned the property and had started out asking over $300,000.00 for it. The previous owner had paid close to $600,000.00 for it. I believe it was reduced to $150,000.00 and had been on the bank's books for over three years. When a building sets empty for a long time it starts to deteriorate, thieves break in and steal the copper wiring from the plumbing and air conditioning and the overgrowth takes over the outside. We initially offered $50,000.00 and were turned down. We went back and offered $75,000.00 and they accepted. However, the purchase depended on whether or not we could get the zoning changed. We understood the prior business had a bar and served quite a bit of alcohol, but that didn't really bother us. We would just cast out the spirit of alcohol. Now, we thought we had gotten the understanding of the Lord, but this was going to be one of His "But God" moments to get us to where He really wanted us to be.

The property was zoned I2, Industrial District, and we needed it changed to IS, Institutional District. We filed an application with the City of Richmond Zoning Board in September of 2018 to acquire the appropriate zoning. We thought by October we'd be moved into our new location and praising God. That did not happen and would be the first in a long line of requirements and denials for zoning change.

We decided if we couldn't get that building to be rezoned we would buy the property surrounding it and build there. Once again we were halted with requirements and rezoning denials.

To our surprise we found out the City of Richmond had already received a grant to develop all of that property for a Certified Technology Park, a TIF area and an Economic Revitalization Area. As it turns out we had been jumping through hoops and spending money when the city had no intention of ever allowing us to have a Church on any of that property. So we washed our hands of that property. "But God" was leading us.

We had started looking for other parcels of land. The third location we chose is at 1817 Highland Road, also in Richmond, Indiana. There isn't enough land to erect the Church/NCC Headquarters we are planning but it has good visibility on Interstate 70 and there is a house that could be converted into an office, a place for visiting ministers to stay while in town or possible a second, smaller Church for discipleship classes for youth. Once again we needed to rezone this property and once again we were turned down. As of this day we have purchased this property and we are working on what we want to do with it.

Prior to "But God" moments are not pleasant or easy, but they are necessary. They are for us to understand that God wants to give us a deeper desire to have a Godly understanding. These "But God" moments are His way of guiding us, directing us, training us, teaching us and showing us His way. We are not to lean on our own understanding. I would have fought to the end for the rezoning on Progress Drive; "But God" stepped in and let us know that He was in charge. Our understanding is nothing compared to His understanding and His ways.

We also found two parcels of joined land just off of Interstate 70, about three miles west of the Highland Road property and a ½ mile north of Progress Drive; 2701 & 2707 Williamsburg Pike, also in Richmond, Indiana.

This was another fight for rezoning. We went through rezoning meetings, numerous requirements from the City Planner's office and eventually we decided to hire a lawyer to represent us. Still we were denied by the City Planner and the Zoning Committee, however, after meeting with all of the City Council members that would meet with us and hear our plea, in May of 2019 we were finally approved for a zoning change for the Williamsburg Pike properties.

"BUT GOD" showed up again! We are now working on 1817 Highland Road and 2701 - 2707 Williamsburg Pike transforming them into meeting our ministry needs.

We will soon be asking the city's Planning Commission and the City Council to change the zoning of 1817 Highland Road from AG zoning, agricultural, to IS zoning, institutional. In the meantime, we will develop the land as agricultural. We even intend to keep some chickens on that parcel of property. Though, we know that we know this is the site God has given us to build our second Church. We are believing for a miracle; we are going to develop it from raising chickens to raising a soul-saving Church.

Chapter Fifteen

By a String on a Map

"The steps of a good man are ordered by the Lord: and he delighteth in his way." **(Psalms 37:23, KJV).**

We have been very fortunate to have several "But God" people in our county and surrounding counties. People, such as, Dr. Raymond Rothwell who also happens to be my pastor and the retired pastor of Full Gospel Temple of Eaton, Ohio; Pastor Kenneth Harbaum, a past youth camper at New Creations Chapel and current Sr. Pastor of Covenant of Peace in Eaton, Ohio; Pastor Carlos King, former staff member at New Creations chapel and Sr. Pastor at Assembly of God in Richmond, Indiana. These and other Men and women of God have changed the course of our Wayne County, Indiana and Preble County, Ohio areas.

Another such man and the one I will focus on is Dr. Frank Holman. He came to Richmond in 1964, from Michigan, with a burning desire to win people to our Lord and Savior, Jesus Christ. A "But God" man who would not give up, give in, or quit to the world's way.

By a string on a map, God called Dr. Frank & Amy Holman and their family to Richmond, Indiana. In the early days it was rough, but this forth standing family would not succumb when on some Sundays it was just their immediate family attending Church.

I was a young man when Dr. Holman came to town claiming he was going to start a Church for the lost sinners of our town. I heard people say, "Dr. Holman and Hillcrest Baptist Church aren't going to make it in this town; they preach hell and they are trying to get 'lost' people 'saved'."

You know all those people who said things about Hillcrest Baptist Church and the Holman family didn't realize the Holman's were "But God" people. The Holman's were not going to be moved by words or accusations about them or their Church. This was a family where God was going to have the last word.

Many people didn't know the Holman's and their little flock had a mind to work and build a Church that would end up winning thousands to Jesus Christ! Their Church people reminded me of those in Jeremiah. *"So built we the wall; and all the wall was joined together unto the half thereof: for the people had a mind to work."* **(Nehemiah 4:6, KJV).**

The flock and their leaders had their minds set to build Hillcrest Baptist Church for the glory of God.

When I met Dr. Holman I fell in love with his vision to win our area for the cause of Jesus Christ. I loved his preaching and was so thankful to be able to be of assistance. I helped Hillcrest Baptist Church secure the property where they are currently located.

After residing in a cramped Church on Sheridan Street they were able to build a new, bigger Church and move to their present location on Hillcrest Drive, just off of State Road 38, North West of the city of Richmond.

There had been a lot of, what I call, pit moments, for the Church and the Holman family while they were constructing the new Church building; not unlike Joseph in Genesis. *"And it came to pass, when Joseph was come unto his brethren, that they stript Joseph out of his coat, his coat of many colours that was on him; And they took him, and cast him into a pit: and the pit was empty, there was no water in it."* **(Genesis 37:23-24, KJV)**.

What encouraged me was, they would have a pit moment in a financial area, where people would think this Church is completely finished. Yet, time and time again they would have a "But God" moment and a miracle would occur.

As I watched Dr. Holman and the Church going through their pit moments it taught me some things. I learned that if you were in a pit like Joseph, you were going to have some "But God" moments. These "But God" moments will rescue you from pits, problems, troubles, lack of finances and many other difficulties. You dare not give up because a "But God" moment is on the way to those who stay the course.

I was overwhelmed as they built Hillcrest Baptist Church with the sheer determination and leading of God to keep them going through the storms, the storms of getting a loan, getting the required down payment for the loan, and getting volunteers to help build the Church.

One great man that I met during that time was Theron Jennings. He was a "But God" man who came in and picked up Hillcrest Baptist Church during some of those tough pit moments by volunteering his skills and time to help build the Church. This man was God sent and God did not just send in an average builder. He sent in a man with golden hands. I would later witness this man with knowledge and ability that could handle the most difficult construction problems. He was a man who would not stop until he got the job done.

After completing Hillcrest Baptist Church, Theron Jennings came to New Creations and was a "But God" man their also. When we needed him, God sent him to us. He and his 'golden hands' volunteered at New Creations for over ten years. He worked over 40 hours a week and did things which could never have been accomplished had he not answered that "But God" call to step in and rescue a sinking ship in our many building projects.

One such project was the water pit at NCCI for city water. For days Theron would literally be working in a pit measuring 4' x 6' x 5'. Finally after weeks of being in that pit he finished hooking up all the pipes and he made his final ascent out of that pit. It not only amazed me, but the building inspectors and the water company management as well.

See, I learned at the Hillcrest Baptist Church that God would send you a "But God" man or woman to rescue you in your time of troubles, if your heart was right and you desired to do a work for God. No devil, or his group of ineffective minions, can stop a "But God" ministry in the quest to bring people to Jesus Christ and to bring glory to God.

"Let your light so shine before men, that they will see your good works, and glorify your Father which is in heaven." **(Matthew 5:16, KJV)**.

At Hillcrest Baptist Church that verse became real to me. If you were doing something for the glory of God our Father it was guaranteed that you would have "But God" moments in your times of trouble. You would defeat the very mind boggling attack from our enemy, the devil.

Those people at Hillcrest, who many pronounced would not make it, would have "But God" moments and be rescued from their pits.

Then the Holman's did what I call a guarantee for many pit moments. They started a Christian School. I witnessed people trying to buy seats on the board only to be told 'no' even when it meant the Church would lose future donations. Dr. Holman had decided God was going to be in charge or there would be no school. Many parents tried to run the school; "But God" was there. God would either bring a "But God" moment or they would have to close the school and the Church.

Finally, like New Creations Christian School, the day came to close Hillcrest's school, or the Church would not survive. What an emotional moment for the "But God" people of Hillcrest Baptist Church. But again, they overcame and the Church was resurrected.

One of the highlights of the "But God" movement at Hillcrest was when Dr. Holman left to go back to Michigan in 1987. How the Church survived those years with the Pastors that tried to replace him was nothing short of "But God" moments.

Then, after Dr. Holman's retirement from Michigan Bible College in 1993, the Church was down to one Sunday with only ten people in the morning service. Dr. Holman was persuaded out of retirement and brought back to rebuild the church congregation. That was yet one more "But God" moment.

I had the privilege to preach Dr. Holman's 80th and 90th birthday Sundays and those were "But God" moments in my life. I also got to preach for the Holman's 70th wedding anniversary as well as the Churches 54th Church anniversary. What a privilege and joy it was to do that for that great man and woman of God.

To me, the Holman's and Hillcrest Baptist Church are like the Old and New

Testament's men and women of God such as, Joseph, Esther, Ruth, Job, Abraham, Martha, Paul and Peter. I thank them for all they taught me while I attended Hillcrest Baptist Church.

"I have planted, Apollos watered; but God gave the increase." **(1 Corinthians 3:6, KJV).**

Yes, Dr. Frank & Amy planted and watered by teaching us about the Godhead, God the Father; God the Son, Jesus Christ and God the Holy Ghost. It was all those "But God" moments in their lives that would teach me that God had to give the increase. It was God who would start and close His ministry.

It was God who would take us to new heights and places through our "But God" moments.

Our family was blessed in 1971 at Hillcrest when 17 of our family members came to know Jesus Christ as their Lord and Savior.

You might wonder how I got the strength to stand in times when no one, including myself, thought I could. Dr. Holman is just one of the men of God who taught me to stand until I had a "But God" moment that would change the course of my life and that of many others for the cause of Jesus Christ.

I am thankful to the Holman's sons, Pastor Martin, Pastor Michael and Pastor Matthew for being there when I was a young Christian and helping me to grow in the Lord. The Holman family are truly "But God" people and have gone through great difficulties for the cause of Christ.

If you have never received Jesus Christ as Lord of your life, your Savior, then you never became a born again Christian. You've been pretty lonely in your troubled times and its time you have a "But God" moment. The changing course of your life can lead many other people to Jesus Christ.

All you have to do is ask Jesus to come into your life and surrender to Him. In our current times I've heard people claim there is more than one way to God but Jesus is the only way to God. *"Jesus saith unto him, I am the way, the truth, and the life: no man cometh unto the Father, but by me."* **(John 14:6, KJV).**

Jesus is waiting for you to ask Him into your life so you can have salvation. He is a gentleman He will not push His way in, you must invite Him in. *"Behold I stand at the door and knock: if any man hear my voice, and open the door, I will come in to him, and will sup with him, and he with me."* **(Revelation 3:20, KJV).**

Realize you are a sinner and ask Jesus to forgive your sins and repent to Him. *"For all have sinned, and come short of the glory of God;"*
(Romans 3:23, KJV).

Realize what sin is and what it does to you. *"For the wages of sin is death; but the gift of God is eternal life through Jesus Christ our Lord."* **(Romans 6:23, KJV).**

Realize how much God loves you and accept it. *"For God so loved the world, that he gave his only begotten Son, that whosoever believeth in him shall not perish, but have everlasting life."* **(John 3:16, KJV)**.

All you have to do is confess and believe. *"That if thou shalt confess with thy mouth the Lord Jesus, and shalt believe in thine heart that God hath raised him from the dead, thou shalt be saved."* **(Romans 10:9-10, KJV)**.

Then you can say that God raised you from the wages of sin and you have become a "But God" man or woman of God! *"But God raised him from the dead:"* **(Acts 13-30, KJV)**.

Jesus will become the "But God" in your troubled times and you will live a victorious life in Christ Jesus!

Index

1. But God came to Abimelech in a dream by night, and said to him, Behold, thou art but a dead man, for the woman which thou hast taken; for she is a man's wife. (Genesis 20:3, KJV).
2. And your father hath deceived me, and changed my wages ten times; but God suffered him not to hurt me. (Genesis 31:7, KJV).
3. So now it was not you that sent me hither, but God: and he hath made me a father to Pharaoh, and lord of all his house, and a ruler throughout all the land of Egypt. (Genesis 45:8, KJV).
4. And Israel said unto Joseph, Behold, I die: but God shall be with you, and bring you again unto the land of your fathers. (Genesis 48:21, KJV).
5. But as for you, ye thought evil against me; but God meant it unto good, to bring to pass, as it is this day, to save much people alive. (Genesis 50:20, KJV).
6. But God led the people about, through the way of the wilderness of the Red sea: and the children of Israel went up harnessed out of the land of Egypt. (Exodus 13:18, KJV).
7. And if a man lie not in wait, but God deliver him into his hand; then I will appoint thee a place whither he shall flee. (Exodus 21:13, KJV).
8. But God clave an hollow place that was in the jaw, and there came water thereout; and when he had drunk, his spirit came again, and he revived: wherefore he called the name thereof Enhakkore, which is in Lehi unto this day. (Judges 15:19, KJV).
9. And David abode in the wilderness in strong holds, and remained in a mountain in the wilderness of Ziph. And Saul sought him every day, but God delivered him not into his hand. (1 Samuel 23:14, KJV).
10. But God said unto me, Thou shalt not build an house for my name, because thou hast been a man of war, and hast shed blood. (1 Chronicles 28:3, KJV).
11. And he said, Hearken ye, all Judah, and ye inhabitants of Jerusalem, and thou king Jehoshaphat, Thus saith the LORD unto you, Be not afraid nor dismayed by

reason of this great multitude; for the battle is not yours, but God's. (2 Chronicles 20:15, KJV).

12. But God will redeem my soul from the power of the grave: for he shall receive me. Selah. (Psalms 49:15, KJV).

13. But God shall shoot at them with an arrow; suddenly shall they be wounded. (Psalms 64:7, KJV).

14. But God shall wound the head of his enemies, and the hairy scalp of such an one as goeth on still in his trespasses. (Psalms 68:21, KJV).

15. My flesh and my heart faileth: but God is the strength of my heart, and my portion for ever. (Psalms 73:26, KJV).

16. But God is the judge: he putteth down one, and setteth up another. (Psalms 75:7, KJV).

17. The righteous man wisely considereth the house of the wicked: but God overthroweth the wicked for their wickedness. (Proverbs 21:12, KJV).

18. The nations shall rush like the rushing of many waters: but God shall rebuke them, and they shall flee far off, and shall be chased as the chaff of the mountains before the wind, and like a rolling thing before the whirlwind. (Isaiah 17:13, KJV).

19. But God prepared a worm when the morning rose the next day, and it smote the gourd that it withered. (Jonah 4:7, KJV).

20. Why doth this man thus speak blasphemies? who can forgive sins but God only? (Mark 2:7, KJV).

21. And the scribes and the Pharisees began to reason, saying, Who is this which speaketh blasphemies? Who can forgive sins, but God alone? (Luke 5:21, KJV).

22. But God said unto him, Thou fool, this night thy soul shall be required of thee: then whose shall those things be, which thou hast provided? (Luke 12:20, KJV).

23. And he said unto them, Ye are they which justify yourselves before men; but God knoweth your hearts: for that which is highly esteemed among men is abomination in the sight of God. (Luke 16:15, KJV).

24. And the patriarchs, moved with envy, sold Joseph into Egypt: but God was with him, (Acts 7:9, KJV).

25. And he said unto them, Ye know how that it is an unlawful thing for a man that is a Jew to keep company, or come unto one of another nation; but God hath shewed me that I should not call any man common or unclean. (Acts 10:28, KJV).

26. But God raised him from the dead: (Acts 13:30, KJV).

27. But God commendeth his love toward us, in that, while we were yet sinners, Christ died for us. (Romans 5:8, KJV).

28. But God be thanked, that ye were the servants of sin, but ye have obeyed from the heart that form of doctrine which was delivered you. (Romans 6:17, KJV).

29. But God hath chosen the foolish things of the world to confound the wise; and God hath chosen the weak things of the world to confound the things which are mighty; (1 Corinthians 1:27, KJV).

30. But God hath revealed them unto us by his Spirit: for the Spirit searcheth all things, yea, the deep things of God. (1 Corinthians 2:10, KJV).

31. I have planted, Apollos watered; but God gave the increase. (1 Corinthians 3:6, KJV)

32. So then neither is he that planteth any thing, neither he that watereth; but God that giveth the increase. (1 Corinthians 3:7, KJV).

33. Meats for the belly, and the belly for meats: but God shall destroy both it and them. Now the body is not for fornication, but for the Lord; and the Lord for the body. (1 Corinthians 6:13, KJV).

34. But if the unbelieving depart, let him depart. A brother or a sister is not under bondage in such cases: but God hath called us to peace. (1 Corinthians 7:15, KJV).

35. There hath no temptation taken you but such as is common to man: but God is faithful, who will not suffer you to be tempted above that ye are able; but will with the temptation also make a way to escape, that ye may be able to bear it. (1 Corinthians 10:13, KJV).

36. For our comely parts have no need: but God hath tempered the body together, having given more abundant honour to that part which lacked. (1 Corinthians 12:24, KJV).

37. But God giveth it a body as it hath pleased him, and to every seed his own body. (1 Corinthians 15:38, KJV).

38. For if the inheritance be of the law, it is no more of promise: but God gave it to Abraham by promise. (Galatians 3:18, KJV).

39. Now a mediator is not a mediator of one, but God is one. (Galatians 3:20, KJV).

40. But God forbid that I should glory, save in the cross of our Lord Jesus Christ, by whom the world is crucified unto me, and I unto the world. (Galatians 6:14, KJV).

41. But God, who is rich in mercy, for his great love wherewith he loved us, (Ephesians 2:4, KJV).

42. For indeed he was sick nigh unto death: but God had mercy on him; and not on him only, but on me also, lest I should have sorrow upon sorrow. (Philippians 2:27, KJV).

43. But as we were allowed of God to be put in trust with the gospel, even so we speak; not as pleasing men, but God, which trieth our hearts. (1 Thessalonians 2:4, KJV).

44. He therefore that despiseth, despiseth not man, but God, who hath also given unto us his holy Spirit. (1 Thessalonians 4:8, KJV).

References

Dake's Annotated Reference Bible
Dake's Publishing, Inc.
PO Box 1050
Lawrenceville, Georgia 30046

The Holy Bible
Containing the Old and New Testaments of the
authorized or
King James Version Text

The Application Study Bible
New Living Translation
copyright 1996
Tynedale House Publishers, Inc.
Wheaton, Illinois 60189. All rights reserved.